James Parton

Colonial pioneers

Governor Bradford. William Brewster. Thomas Hutchinson. Lord
Baltimore. Peter Stuyvesant. William Johnson.

James Parton

Colonial pioneers
Governor Bradford. William Brewster. Thomas Hutchinson. Lord Baltimore. Peter Stuyvesant. William Johnson.

ISBN/EAN: 9783337175153

Printed in Europe, USA, Canada, Australia, Japan

Cover: Foto ©ninafisch / pixelio.de

More available books at **www.hansebooks.com**

GOVERNOR BRADFORD.	WILLIAM JOHNSON.
WILLIAM BREWSTER.	JAMES LOGAN.
THOMAS HUTCHINSON.	CAPTAIN KIDD.
LORD BALTIMORE.	REV. SAMUEL PARRIS.
PETER STUYVESANT.	CAPT. HENRY HUDSON.

BY

JAMES PARTON,

AUTHOR OF

" LIFE OF HORACE GREELEY," " LIFE OF ANDREW JACKSON," " LIFE AND TIMES OF BENJAMIN FRANKLIN," ETC. ETC.

With Introduction.

NEW YORK:

Effingham Maynard & Co., Publishers,

771 BROADWAY AND 67 & 69 NINTH STREET,

INTRODUCTION.

JAMES PARTON was born in Canterbury, England, February 9, 1822. When five years old he was brought to America and given an education in the schools of New York City, and at White Plains, N. Y. Subsequently he engaged in teaching in Philadelphia and New York City, and for three years was a contributor to the *Home Journal*. Since that time, he has devoted his life to literary labors, contributing many articles to periodicals and publishing books on biographical subjects. While employed on the *Home Journal* it occurred to him that an interesting story could be made out of the life of Horace Greeley, and he mentioned the idea to a New York publisher. Receiving the needed encouragement, Mr. Parton set about collecting material from Greeley's former neighbors in Vermont and New Hampshire, and in 1855 produced the " Life of Horace Greeley," which he afterwards extended and completed in 1885. This venture was so profitable that he was encouraged to devote himself to authorship. In 1856 he brought out a collection of Humorous Poetry of the English Language from Chaucer to Saxe. Following this appeared in 1857 the " Life of Aaron Burr," prepared from original sources and intended to redeem Burr's reputation from the charges that attached to his memory. In writing the " Life of Andrew Jackson " he also had access to original and unpublished documents. This work was published in three volumes in 1859–60. Other works of later publication are: " General Butler in New Orleans " (1863 and 1882); " Life and Times of Benjamin Franklin " (1864); " How New York is Governed " (1866); "Famous Americans of

3

Recent Times," containing Sketches of Henry Clay, Daniel Webster, John C. Calhoun, John Randolph, and others (1867); " The People's Book of Biography," containing eighty short lives (1868); " Smoking and Drinking," an essay on the evils of those practices, reprinted from the *Atlantic Monthly* (1869); a pamphlet entitled " The Danish Islands: Are We Bound to Pay for Them?" (1869); " Topics of the Time," a collection of magazine articles, most of them treating of administrative abuses at Washington (1871); " Triumphs of Enterprise, Ingenuity, and Public Spirit " (1871); " The Words of Washington " (1872); " Fanny Fern," a memorial volume (1873); " Life of Thomas Jefferson, Third President of the United States " (1874); " Taxation of Church Property " (1874); " La Parnasse Français: a Book of French Poetry from A.D. 1850 to the Present Time " (1877); " Caricature and other Comic Art in All Times and Many Lands " (1877); " A Life of Voltaire," which was the fruit of several years' labor (1881); " Noted Women of Europe and America " (1883); and " Captains of Industry, or Men of Business who did something besides Making Money: a Book for Young Americans." In addition to his writing Mr. Parton has proved a very successful lecturer on literary and political topics.

In January, 1856, Mr. Parton married Sara Payson Willis, a sister of the poet N. P. Willis, and herself famous as " Fanny Fern," the name of her pen. He made New York City his home until 1875, three years after the death of his wife, when he went to Newburyport, where he now lives. *The London Athenæum* well characterizes Mr. Parton as " a painstaking, honest, and courageous historian, ardent with patriotism, but unprejudiced; a writer, in short, of whom the people of the United States have reason to be proud."

The contents of this book have been selected from among the great number contributed from time to time by Mr. Parton, and are considered as particularly valuable and interesting reading.

Colonial Pioneers.

Governor William Bradford,

The First Historian of the Pilgrim Fathers in New England.

In the year 1606, William Bradford, a sickly English youth of sixteen, was accustomed to walk by a foot-path through the fields every Sunday, from his native village Austerfield, to attend a religious service at the house of William Brewster in the village of Scrooby. The reader may think this an unimportant circumstance to mention; but many sons of New England, while traveling in old England, have gone a long distance out of their way to visit those villages, and tread the path by which young Bradford made his way to Brewster's house. It was a walk of three or four miles. Austerfield is now a village of thirty brick houses, two of which, it is said, look as if they might have been standing in Bradford's day; and the little church in which he was baptized is still standing, and contains many objects that have undergone no alteration since.

Left an orphan at an early age, he was taken home by his grandfather, who designed to bring him up a farmer, like himself and all his ancestors from time immemorial. His bodily strength being unequal to hard labor, he spent a great portion of his youth in study, and thus became conversant with the Latin and Greek authors, whom he frequently quotes in his writings.

The ministers of the Established Church, at that time, had become, many of them, incredibly degraded in mind and morals—to the great grief and disgust of such as this thoughtful and studious youth. The minister of Austerfield was even unusually ignorant and licentious. William Bradford, therefore, who had imbibed the principles of the Puritans, joined the little congregation which gathered at Scrooby. Many of his neighbors and some of his nearest relations laughed at him, and called him Puritan, which was then a term of reproach; but he held on his way in spite of ridicule and opposition. Despised by the ignorant populace, and hunted down by the government, the Scrooby congregation were frequently obliged to change their place of meeting, and, though using every precaution, they were liable, whenever they met, to be seized, cast into prison, and heavily fined.

The patience of these worthy people was at length exhausted. Or, to use the language of William Bradford:

"So, after they had continued together about a year, and kept their meetings every Sabbath, in one place or other, exercising the worship of God among themselves, notwithstanding all the diligence and malice of their adversaries, they, seeing they could no longer continue in that condition, resolved to get over into Holland as they could."

It was a desperate resolution, and one that evidently struck their friends with amazement. All of them, except the minister and one or two others, were farmers, unacquainted with any other trade or business, and singularly unfitted to earn their livelihood in a country like Holland, where the language, customs, and occupations of the people were all equally strange and foreign to them. Bradford himself, though his parents had left him a considerable estate, possessed nothing, because he was not yet of age; nor could he expect help from his uncles, with whom he then lived, for they hated the Puritans. Nevertheless the youth had cast in his lot with the church at Scrooby, and he determined to go with them.

The enterprise was the more difficult, because the king had forbidden the Non-conformists to leave the country, and no spy was more welcome to the Tory magistrates of the time than one who came to give information of innocent people designing to abandon England for such a reason as theirs. The seaport most convenient for their purpose was Boston, in Lincolnshire, about forty miles distant from Scrooby. This poor company of farmers, after selling their household goods as best they could, concealing the act from hostile neighbors, were obliged to procure secret means of conveyance to Boston; and while hiding there, to bribe the captains of vessels to secrecy, and offer extortionate rates for a passage. Several times, Governor Bradford states, when they had paid their passage, and made every arrangement for their departure, their captain betrayed them, and left them and their goods the prey of the king's officers. One instance of this nature he relates in a most simple and affecting manner.

After many disappointments, a large company of them, one of whom was Bradford himself, hired a whole ship, and a time was appointed for their coming on board. In the darkness of the night they left their hiding-places in Boston, bearing with them their personal effects, and rowed off to the vessel lying at anchor in the stream. This captain also was a traitor. The king's officers came on board the next day; "who took them," says Bradford, "and put them into open boats, and there rifled and ransacked them, searching them to their shirts for money; yea, even the women further than became modesty; and then carried them back into the town, and made them a spectacle and wonder to the multitude, which came flocking on all sides to behold them."

Robbed thus of their money, books, and apparel, they were carried before the magistrates; by whom they were committed to prison. After a month's imprisonment, they were all dismissed except seven, one of whom was Bradford; and these leaders of the fugitives were kept in prison until the next court. Before they were released the winter was well advanced, and these poor, innocent people, who had then no homes of their own, lived during the rest of the rigorous season in the homes of their friends about Scrooby.

Undismayed, they renewed the attempt in the spring, this time hiring a Dutch ship, hoping to find a Dutch captain more faithful than those of their own nation. On the shores of the broad Humber, not far from the town of Great Grimsby, there was a lonely place suitable for their purpose, where the Dutch captain agreed to meet them on a certain day, and take them on board his vessel. As the time drew near, the company gathered at Hull, a city on the other side of the Humber, and about fifteen miles distant from the place agreed upon.

When the day came the women and children were placed on board a small vessel at Hull, and conveyed to the rendezvous, while the men crossed the Humber at Hull, and made their way by land. When the women arrived there was no ship in sight; and as they were sick with the roughness of the sea, they begged the sailors to put into a creek near by, where their boat would be at ease. The sailors complied with their request, and in the course of the night the tide fell and left them aground. In the morning the ship arrived; but the women could not stir until the tide rose. To save time, the Dutch captain sent his boat to get the men aboard whom he saw ready and walking about the shore. One boat-load was got safely on board the vessel, but just as the boat was ready to push off for

---

another load, the captain saw a great company of armed men, horse and foot, coming to capture his passengers.

"Sacrament!" cried the Dutchman, swearing the familiar oath of his country, and instantly weighed his anchor, and put to sea with a fair wind.

It is difficult to say which of the forlorn party were most to be pitied—the men on board the vessel, borne away from their wives and children, the women left hard and fast in the middle of the creek, or the men who had to run and make their escape from the troops. Bradford, to his honor be it said, and a few others, staid to assist the women in their agony.

"Pitiful it was," he says, "to see the heavy case of these poor women in this distress; what weeping and crying on every side; some for their husbands that were carried away in the ship; others not knowing what should become of them and their little ones; others, again, melted in tears, seeing their poor little ones hanging about them crying for fear and quaking with cold."

The helpless women were seized by the troopers; but, after being hurried from one place to another, and from court to court, they were released, and found their way to places of refuge. The interruption of the embarkation proved to be a fortunate circumstance, for there arose soon after so violent a storm, and one of such long continuance, that if all the company had been on board the little vessel, it would in all probability have gone to the bottom. Fortunately too, Brewster, Robinson, Clifford, Bradford, and other influential persons of the company remained in England, and through their exertions the little congregation found their way to Holland, and the distracted families were reunited. Brewster and Robinson, it appears, like the faithful captain and mate of a ship, would not leave England until the last of the company were embarked.

In Holland, as Bradford eloquently says, the poor pilgrims saw "fair and beautiful cities, flowing with abundance of all sorts of wealth and riches;" but in those riches these English farmers had no part; and "it was not long before they saw the grim and grisly face of poverty coming upon them like an armed man, with whom they must buckle and encounter, and from whom they could not fly."

But they went to work, like men of sense, at whatever honest thing they could find to do. At Leyden, where they settled, Robinson, their minister, wrote and translated books; Brewster gave lessons in English to the students of the University; Bradford became a silk weaver, and, by and by, when he came of age, he sold his inheritance in England, and invested it in the silk business. He prospered so well that he married in Holland, and was able to contribute something to the assistance of his poorer brethren; others of the congregation became hatters; others workers in wool; and some engaged in more laborious mechanical trades.

When, twelve years after settling in Holland, the pilgrims emigrated to Plymouth in Massachusetts, Bradford went with them, and he became the second governor of the colony, serving it for many years with wisdom, courage, and fidelity. Toward the close of his life he wrote that invaluable history of the Plymouth Plantation, by which it is chiefly known. He died in 1657, aged sixty-nine, "lamented," as Cotton Mather observes, "by all the colonies of New England, as a common blessing and father to them all."

Some books have a history as strange as the events which they record: and this was the case with the one written by William Bradford. It was lost for a hundred years, and was then discovered where no one would have thought of looking for the manuscript history of an American colony. Every one who has had occasion to look into the early history of New England, is aware that the oldest books relating to the Plymouth colony frequently refer to Governor Bradford's History of Plymouth, and draw from it some of their most interesting information. In 1758, we know that it was deposited in the tower of the Old South Church in Boston, along with other precious works, both printed and manuscript; but from that time nothing was heard of it until within these few years. As the Old South Church, during the Revolutionary war, was used as a riding school by the British troops, it was feared that Bradford's History had been destroyed or carried off by some one ignorant of its value.

In 1855, the Rev. John S. Barry, who was engaged in writing a history of Massachusetts, observed, while reading the Bishop of Oxford's History of the Episcopal Church in America, that the author quoted passages from Bradford, which, he stated, were derived from "a manuscript History of the Plantation of Plymouth, in the Fulham library." Fulham is a suburb of London, where the Bishops of London have their summer residence. This led to the discovery of the manuscript. It was found in the library of the Bishop of London, where it had been, no one knew how long, and where the Bishop had discovered it when searching for material for his work upon the history named above. The Historical Society of Massachusetts caused an exact copy of it to be made, which was published in 1856. Of all the documents relating to the early history of New England, this is by far the most interesting.

William Brewster and the Pilgrims in England.

In the English county of Nottingham, on the high road from London to Edinburgh, at a point about one hundred and fifty miles from the English capital, is the ancient village named Scrooby. The parish contains less than three hundred inhabitants, farmers most of them, and the village is only a small cluster of houses gathered near one of those beautiful old churches which give such charm and dignity to English rural landscapes.

A quarter of a mile from Scrooby church there is a farm-house which once formed part of a stately mansion belonging to the Archbishop of York ; but which, in the latter part of the reign of Queen Elizabeth, had lost much of its grandeur, and had come to be the residence of a gentleman farmer, named William Brewster. The mansion has now disappeared, except that a part of its stables, or some other out-building, has been converted into the farm-house just mentioned. The mansion, in the day of its glory, was surrounded by a moat, the line of which can still be traced in the indented soil.

William Brewster, who lived in this house, was a Puritan of some learning, and much experience in the great affairs of the world. After a short residence at the University of Cambridge, he made his way to court, where he obtained in due time a confidential clerkship under one of the secretaries of state, Davison, an eminent Puritan of the time. Brewster used to accompany the secretary when he waited upon the queen, and once when he went upon an embassy to Holland ; and thus he became familiar with one of the few spots in Europe which then enjoyed a measure of religious liberty.

It was Davidson, the reader may remember, who issued the warrant for the execution of Mary Queen of Scots, an act which had the hearty approval of the intelligent and well-informed Puritans of England. In accordance with her timid and tortuous policy, Elizabeth feigned to be offended with the secretary of state for issuing the warrant, and dismissed him from his office, which deprived William Brewster also of his place.

Brewster soon after retired to his native Nottinghamshire, and took up his abode in the archbishop's vacant manor-house, at Scrooby. His income during his long residence there was derived in part, as I conjecture, from invested property, and partly from the cultivation of land; and he derived some emolument from the office of postmaster, which his patron may have procured for him. Not that he was a village postmaster, in the modern sense of the term, but rather a master of one of the posts between London and Edinburgh, where couriers and post-riders obtained fresh horses, leaving perhaps behind them a letter or two for some important personage of the county. In a word, William Brewster was a man of substance and respectability, a leading person in his parish, and held in particular respect as a gentleman who had been at Court, and served one of the queen's ministers both at home and abroad.

Like his old master, the secretary of state. William Brewster was a Puritan; in other words, he was a person who preferred a plain and simple form of worship, without imposing rites or vestments, to the ornate and elaborate ceremonial ordained by Queen Elizabeth. *Preferred* is an insufficient word to express the feelings of the more advanced Puritans. As the queen became more exacting in her demands, the Puritans grew more scrupulous; until what had first been a preference, became a conviction for which they were willing to peril liberty and life. In the latter part of Elizabeth's reign, an act of Parliament was passed declaring that any one who neglected to come to the Established Church for a month, or attended any religious service other than that of the Church of England, should be imprisoned until they should recant, and promise compliance with the law. Those who refused to conform were liable to banishment from the realm for life, under penalty of death if they presumed to visit their native land.

This law, however, during the last five years of the queen's reign, was not so vigorously enforced but that, in all large towns, and in many rural villages, congregations of Non-conformists gathered on Sunday without any great precautions as to secrecy, and joined in such a simple religious service as their consciences approved. Many excellent clergymen, however, were expelled from their livings, and several men of learning suffered death or long imprisonment for writings adverse to the observances of the national church. There was just enough persecution to give to Puritanism the additional charm of forbidden fruit. There was enough to advertise and glorify, but not enough to crush it.

When Elizabeth died in 1603, and James I. was proclaimed in her stead, the Puritans rejoiced, for the new king had been reared a Presbyterian, and had been much addicted to arguing, in his arbitrary and pretentious manner, against Episcopacy. He was thirty-six years of age when he came to the throne of England, and it was reasonable to suppose that the opinions which he had cherished so long, as king of Scotland, he would at least respect and tolerate as king of Great Britain.

The Puritans were disappointed. On his way to London, eight hundred clergymen joined in petitioning him to abolish the surplice, the ring in marriage, the use of the cross in baptism, and the rule requiring persons to bow at the name of Jesus. They asked, also, that the Liturgy might be shortened, Sunday more strictly observed, and the other holidays made optional. In short, they asked the king to make the Church of England Puritanic in its rites and observances, while retaining its Episcopal form. The king's reply to this petition was published in the form of a proclamation, announcing his determination to preserve the church as he found it established by law, and forbidding all publications against it. He threw himself and all his influence upon the side of what we should call the High Church party. "No Bishop, no King," said he. In the presence of a number of clergymen, he used these words :

"I will have one doctrine, one discipline, one religion, in substance and ceremony ; never speak more to that point, how far you are bound to obey."

His deed accorded with his words. The Non-conformist congregations were pursued with a rigor unknown in the worst days of Elizabeth ; and not only that, but they were forbidden to seek an asylum in other lands. But for this foolish king, great numbers of persecuted Puritans would have gone to Virginia soon after the settlement of Jamestown in 1607, and Virginia might have become a Puritan commonwealth. Not only were the Puritans prosecuted with new rigor, but all other persons who presumed to differ from the king in their creed or worship. In the year 1611, for example, two men of great worth and learning were executed for professing doctrines precisely similar to those of the late Dr. Channing of Boston, and most of our present Unitarians.

The Puritans, however, increased in numbers and in positiveness of conviction, during every year of the reign of James the First ; and before England was rid of him, we may truly say that they were a majority of the educated class. Consider, for example, this incident, which occurred in Parliament in 1620. A bill being before the House for the more strict observance of Sunday, a member opposed the bill, especially objecting to the day being called *Sabbath*, and declaring his conviction that it was right for people to amuse themselves on Sunday in games and field sports. For this speech he was expelled from the House of Commons, and in the sentence of expulsion his offense is styled, "*great, exorbitant, and unparalleled.*" This action, of course, was aimed at the king, who had made himself profoundly odious to the nation; but it shows that a majority of the House of Commons, in 1620, were at least political, if not religious Puritans.

In several villages near Scrooby there were congregations of Non-conformists in Elizabeth's day. In 1606, the third year of the reign of King James, a company of Puritans assembled at the house of William Brewster, at Scrooby, and formed themselves into a church, in form and doctrine closely resembling what we now call Congregational. The principal member of this church, and its most liberal supporter, was the person at whose house it assembled. Its minister was Richard Clifton, who had been once rector of a church near by, from which he had withdrawn, or been expelled for non-conformity. He was fifty-three years of age when the church was formed, and little else is known of him, except that he was much beloved and trusted by the people to whom he preached. He was assisted in the work of instructing the congregation by John Robinson, who succeeded him in his office, and whose name will be forever famous as pastor of the church of the Pilgrim Fathers when they sailed for the New World in 1620.

Except Brewster, Clifton, and Robinson, all of the congregation were farmers, or persons closely connected with agriculture. At that day, it was not usual for farmers to know how to read and write. Shakespeare's father, for example, who had not been long dead, did not possess these accom-

plishments, though descended from a line of respectable farmers. It is no slight proof, therefore, of the superior-
ity of the persons who met every Sunday at Brewster's
abode, that a large proportion of them could sign their own
names, and read their native language. Theological discus-
sion had sharpened their wits and made them intellectual
beings. Any man who will pursue a great theme in a dis-
interested spirit for several years, weighing the arguments
for and against his own opinion, becomes necessarily an
educated person. He has a mental life, apart from the
daily life of toil and care to which all men are subject,
while they have bodies to nourish and families to rear.

When the church which met at William Brewster's house
had been in existence for about a year, persecution grew so
hot against them that they made up their minds to abandon
their country and seek in another land the rights denied
them in their own. Many Non-conformists from that part
of England, and one whole church from a village near by,
had already found refuge in Holland, which was then almost
the only spot in Europe where religious liberty had an existence. With unconceivable difficulty and suffering the
Scrooby church made its way to Holland, where they re-
sided for twelve years, earning their living by manual labor,
and then emigrated to Plymouth, in Massachusetts.

William Brewster died there in 1643, aged eighty years,
having lived long enough to see, upon the coast of Massachusetts, many thriving settlements of English Puritans.

Thomas Hutchinson,

The Last of the Colonial Governors of Massachusetts.

At the beginning of the Revolutionary War, each of the
American colonies, except Rhode Island, had its governor
who was appointed by the King of England.

The governors' salaries ranged from eight hundred to fifteen hundred pounds per annum, and as the posts were on many accounts highly desirable, they were usually given to court favorites, or to needy hangers-on of the ministry, who continued to live in England, while the service was performed by deputies.

Massachusetts, however, was ruled by a native of the American soil—Thomas Hutchinson—born at Boston in 1711, a graduate of Harvard College, fond of his country, a diligent student of its history, an adherent of its religion, and long held by his fellow-citizens in high esteem.

At the outbreak of the Revolution, he, like all the other royal governors, sided with the king, and contributed materially to aggravate the differences between the colonists and the royal government.

I think it probable that he would have been a royalist in any case, simply because, though not wanting in practical ability, he was a man of dull and limited mind. He was an American George the Third, and naturally assisted that royal personage to muddle away the richest colonial empire a nation ever possessed.

During those trying years Dr. Franklin was puzzled to account for the foolish and fatal proceedings of the British government. He was talking upon this problem one day in London with a member of Parliament, when he received important light upon the matter. The member said, in substance:

" The measures which so offend the people of Massachusetts do not originate with the ministry here, nor in England at all. The sending out of the troops and the other colonial grievances have been suggested and urged by Americans themselves, men in high office, who have written over and over again to the ministry, arguing that nothing but *force* would subdue the American discontent."

Franklin doubted the statement; whereupon the member engaged to prove it, and a few days after brought him a packet of thirteen letters written by Governor Hutchinson Lieutenant-Governor Andrew Oliver, and other persons of note in Boston, to a gentleman connected with the home government. These letters went far to establish the truth of the member's assertion. Six of the worst of them were written by Governor Hutchinson, and they caused Dr. Franklin to open his eyes very wide.

In these epistles the governor spoke of the leading patriots, such as Hancock, Otis, and Samuel Adams, as " our incendiaries." He expressed the opinion that these leaders of the people ought to be brought to trial and punished as criminals. Here are two or three of his most offensive sentences :

" There must be an abridgment of what are called English liberties." " I doubt whether it is possible to project a system of government in which a colony three thousand miles distant from the parent state shall enjoy all the liberty of the parent state." " Laying taxes upon all cannot be thought equal, seeing many will be punished who are not offenders. Penalties of another kind seem better adapted."

The other letters were in the same taste, all agreeing that unless the British government would arrest and convict the " original incendiaries," restrain the liberty of the press and of public meeting, anarchy would continue to prevail.

Upon reading these letters, Franklin's indignation against the government was much allayed, because he saw from them how grossly ministers had been misinformed and misled by persons to whom they naturally looked for correct information. He sent the letters to the Committee of Correspondence in Boston to be shown to the leading patriots. The letters by no means diminished *their* indignation. Indeed, they made the governor so intensely odious that his position was scarcely tenable in the colony. The assembly petitioned the king to remove him and the lieutenant-governor from their posts, since they were "justly chargeable with the corruption, misery, and bloodshed which have been the natural effects of posting an army in a populous town."

The king was little disposed to comply with this request, but in 1774 "gave Governor Hutchinson leave" to visit England. He left Boston not too soon for his own safety, and he spent the remainder of his days in London.

At first he expected to return speedily to his government, and he continued to mislead the king and ministry by assuring them that the troubles would soon be over. In this he deceived himself as much as he did the ministers, for, as before remarked, he was a man who had not the least comprehension of the movement which he had witnessed from the beginning. He understood it as little as King George himself, who was impatient to see his congenial governor. Before he could attire himself in a suitable dress, he received a summons to court, where, notwithstanding his ill-dressed condition, he was "admitted, contrary to custom, to kiss his majesty's hand in his closet." He had a conversation with his majesty of two hours' duration, and was obliged to stand all the time in the Awful Presence of the king.

"I am afraid you are tired, so long standing," said the minister in attendance, at the close of the interview.

"So gracious a reception," replied the governor, "makes me insensible of it."

Upon returning to his lodgings, the governor wrote down his conversation with the king at great length, but the "interview" is by no means interesting or valuable.

"How do you do, Mr. Hutchinson, after your voyage?" asked the king.

"Much reduced, sir, by sea-sickness, and unfit upon that

account, as well as my New England dress, to appear before your majesty."

The king accepted the apology for his clothes, and then asked a great number of gossipy questions about persons and things in Massachusetts, particularly about Hancock, Adams, Cushing, and other noted patriots. He also asked many questions concerning the climate and productions of New England, and appeared to have considerable knowledge of the country himself. The king said:

"Nothing could be more cruel than the treatment you met with in betraying your private letters. I remember nothing in them to which the least exception could be taken. Could you ever find how those letters came to New England?"

"Dr. Franklin, may it please your majesty, has made a public declaration that he sent them."

"I see," said the king, "they threaten to pitch and feather you."

"Tar and feather, may it please your majesty; but I don't remember that ever I was threatened with it."

After two hours of rather trifling talk, the governor withdrew to his abode, perfectly enchanted with the king, who, on his part, was well content with the governor, and continued to pay his salary as long as he lived, and, I believe, gave an office to his son.

It is difficult to tell from the governor's Diary, recently published, which was the strongest feeling of his heart in England—the yearning to return to his native land, or admiration for the English king. He felt himself, as he wrote one day, to be "a prisoner" in old England, " with his heart and affections in New England;" but, on the same day, he wrote in his diary these words:

"I have just come in from the House of Lords, where I saw the king give his assent to one of the American bills, and a number of others. The king is such a figure of a man that, seated on his throne in his royal robes, there is nothing here that affords such a feast to my eyes."

When he penned these words, the news of the battle of Lexington was coming across the sea. Bunker Hill soon followed, and the governor perceived that his stay in England was likely to be long. He lived liberally, however, in England, kept a carriage, visited noblemen at their country seats, attended court, and wrote daily in a Diary which gradually swelled to seven large volumes. During the war his country house in Massachusetts was sacked and pillaged. He did not live to see his country independent, though he lived long enough to hear of Burgoyne's surrender, of the French alliance, and of the beginning of the movements which ended in the capture of Cornwallis.

He died in London in 1780, aged sixty-nine years, leaving children and grandchildren. Peter Orlando Hutchinson, one of his great-grandsons, has begun the publication of his Diary and letters, which have their value, and show the governor to have been as honest as a man of his caliber can ordinarily be. He was, however, quite aware on which side his bread was buttered, and he liked it buttered.

Lord Baltimore and Maryland.

In an English journal of 1771, I read, some time ago, the following paragraph:

"Lord Baltimore's will has come over from Italy. It appears that he has left the province of Maryland, in tail, male, to Henry Harford, Esq., a child now at Richmond

School; remainder in fee to his younger sister, the Hon. Mrs. Eden."

The reader may not understand the precise meaning of the law terms in this paragraph; but he may certainly gather from it that the sovereign state of Maryland, only ninety-nine years ago, was the property of a school-boy, an item in a nobleman's will; and it was by no means the most important item. I could not but think of this when I sailed, not long ago, out of the harbor of Baltimore, on an afternoon when a fresh southerly breeze was wafting toward that flourishing and important city whole fleets of Baltimore clippers, oystermen, and other coasting craft.

The province had then been in the family of Lord Baltimore one hundred and twenty-eight years; but five years after the paragraph was penned, it ceased to be private property. The school-boy, Henry Harford, Esq., never came into his inheritance; for the people of Maryland took their province into their own hands, and sent a fine regiment to join the forces under General Washington, which distinguished itself at the battle of Long Island and elsewhere.

George Calvert, afterward Lord Baltimore, who was born in Yorkshire, England, about 1582, graduated at Oxford when he was only fifteen years of age, and after the usual tour abroad, entered the public service under James I., and rose to the rank of secretary of state. The king, with whom he was a favorite, knighted him, made him a peer of Ireland with the title of Lord Baltimore, and settled upon him a pension of a thousand pounds a year. The town of Baltimore, from which he derived his title, is now a small seaport near Cork, containing a population of less than two hundred persons.

While he was still secretary of state, and when he was fifty-two years of age, a remarkable change took place in his religious opinions. He became a Roman Catholic. He resigned his office in consequence, freely confessing to the king the change which he had experienced. If the king had been a consistent personage, this avowal would have estranged him forever from George Calvert. He had said, not long before:

"I can love the person of a Papist, being otherwise a good man and honestly bred, never having known any other religion; but the person of an apostate Papist I hate."

But he did not hate George Calvert. On the contrary, he kept him in the Privy Council, and manifested in various ways an undiminished regard for him. Released from his office of secretary of state, in 1624, Lord Baltimore had time to carry out a scheme of colonization which he had long had at heart. Some years before King James had given him a patent of part of the island of Newfoundland, and he had spent an immense sum of money in preparing his province for a colony, even building a costly house for himself. The colony was planted at length. In 1625, the death of the king having dissolved the tie which kept Lord Baltimore in his native country, he joined his colony in Newfoundland.

He was not long in discovering that the site was ill-chosen, for the climate was cold and the soil unfertile. He persevered, however, for three years. Then he sailed southward on a voyage of discovery, entered the Chesapeake Bay, ascended the James, the Potomac, and the other waters of the Chesapeake, enchanted at every turn with the magnificence of the waters, and the inviting fertility of the lands. He returned to England, and obtained of the new king, Charles I., a grant of the province lying to the north of the Potomac river, then called Crescentia. The king, in honor of his wife, named it Maryland. But this Lord Baltimore never again trod the soil of the province which had been given him. He died in 1632, bequeathing it to his eldest son, who was zealous to execute his father's intentions, and prepared at once to found a colony.

It is evident that the planting of a colony in America by English Catholics was an event highly interesting to the Catholics of the time. A citizen of Maryland, a few years ago, copied from the records of the Jesuits' college at Rome, a report concerning the enterprise, written before the first vessel had sailed. It was evidently designed as an advertisement of the design, and was probably used to induce Catholics to volunteer. It set forth that " His Most Serene Majesty, in his munificence," had given this noble province to the Lord Baron of Baltimore, and his heirs forever.

" Therefore," continued the Jesuit writer, " the most illustrious baron has resolved immediately to lead a colony into that region; first, and especially, that into the same and the neighboring places he may carry the light of the Gospel where, it has been found out, that hitherto no knowledge of the true God has shone. Then, furthermore, with this design, that all the companions of his voyage and labors may be admitted to a participation of the profits and honor, and that the empire of the realm may be more widely extended. For this enterprise, with all haste and diligence, he seeks companions of his voyage."

He proceeds to say, that whosoever shall pay down one hundred pounds to convey five men to the colony, shall receive a grant of two thousand acres of land. And such land!—land abounding in the most beautiful trees, fruits, vegetables, and grain, as well as with the beasts and birds most useful to man.

" So great," said he, " is the abundance of *swine* and deer, that they are rather troublesome than advantageous. Cows also are innumerable, and oxen, suitable for bearing burdens or for food. . . . The neighboring forests are full of wild bulls and heifers, of which five or six hundred thousand are annually carried to Seville from that part which lies toward New Mexico. . . . There is hope also of finding gold, for the neighboring people wear bracelets of unwrought gold, and long strings or pearls."

It is evident that the Jesuit father, in describing Lord Baltimore's province, drew from Captain John Smith's account of Virginia, and from Spanish descriptions of Florida, Mexico, and the West Indies.

Adventurers were not wanting to sail to so pleasant and bountiful a land. A good company of Catholics, under the governorship of Leonard Calvert, a brother of Lord Baltimore, sailed from the Isle of Wight in November, 1633. There were two or three priests on board, who carried with them all that is necessary for the proper celebration of the Catholic worship. As soon as the anchor was hoisted, and the ship under sail, the priests and people walked in procession about the vessel, and "placed the principal parts of it under the protection of God, the most holy Mother, Saint Ignatius, and all the other guardian angels of Maryland."

Sailors were then such slaves to custom and tradition, that almost every ship which sailed to the new world went round by way of the Azores, and so crossed the Atlantic. This ship, by taking that roundabout course, sailed about nine thousand miles, and consumed three months in getting from the Isle of Wight to old Point Comfort in Virginia. After spending a few days in visiting the Virginia settlements, the ship continued its course up Chesapeake Bay to the river Potomac, to which they gave the name of Saint Gregory. The Indian name, however, refused to be set aside, and it continued to be called by its ancient name.

After sailing up the Potomac some distance, exciting the wonder of the natives—for this vessel of four hundred tons was the largest ever before seen in these waters—they reached three small islands, upon one of which they landed.

There, for the first time in that part of America, March 25, 1634, the mass was celebrated. One of the fathers records that, after the conclusion of the ceremony, they took up on their shoulders a great cross which they had hewn from a tree, and going in procession to the place that had been selected for it, they erected it "as a trophy to Christ the Saviour." While some were engaged in setting up the cross, the governor and the rest of the company knelt upon the virgin soil, never before trodden by civilized man, and "chanted humbly the litany of the holy cross, with great emotion of soul."

After a few days' stay upon this island, they sailed thirty miles further up the river, and, landing upon the Maryland side, selected a spot for their intended city, to which they gave in advance the name of Mary. The county is still called by that name, but the great city of Maryland was destined to rise at another point, and was not founded for nearly a hundred years after.

Thus was the colony of Maryland planted. For several years its growth was slow, and I find it spoken of in the records of the time as a "Mission." The priests, of whom there were generally four or five, exerted themselves unceasingly to instruct and convert the Indians, dealing with them with scrupulous justice, and setting them an excellent example of cheerful industry. One of the fathers relates with exultation that among their converts was the principal chief of the country, who cast aside his skins and put on a Christian coat, and dismissed all his wives but one, to whom the fathers married him.

The Baltimore family, who had themselves suffered from the religious intolerance of the age, early declared and made it a fundamental law of the colony, that all religions should be tolerated in their province, saying that they wished it to be a sanctuary for the oppressed of every creed. This wise

movement, so much in advance of the time, attracted many
emigrants.   In twenty-six years after the planting of the
cross upon the island in the Potomac, there were twelve
thousand white people in Maryland; and eleven years after
there were twenty thousand.   Baltimore, which is destined
to be one of the great cities, not of America only, but of the
world, was not laid out until 1729, and in 1765 was only a
village of sixty houses.

PETER STUYVESANT,
FOURTH GOVERNOR OF NEW NETHERLANDS.

IN the Caribbean Sea, a few miles north of Venezuela,
there is an island, forty miles long and two wide, called
Curaçoa, which produces abundant crops of indigo, sugar,
tobacco, and corn.   This island was captured by the Dutch
in 1634, during their long struggle with Spain for their
national independence, and it remains in their possession to
the present day.   Soon after its capture, an Amsterdam
company of merchants founded a colony there, and carried
on a profitable trade in the products of the island.

The first governor of this colony was Peter Stuyvesant,
afterward so famous as the governor of New Netherlands.
He was the son of a Dutch Calvinistic clergyman, and received the classical education usually enjoyed at that day,
in Holland, by the sons of gentlemen.   He became particularly conversant with the Latin language, and he was fond,
all his life, of quoting Latin sentences, as the manner of
classical scholars then was.   A Dutch author records that
his conduct at school was not too exemplary, but he certainly did not neglect his Latin.   When his school days
were over he entered the army, and after serving some years

he was selected by the West India Company of Amsterdam to be the Governor of their colony at Curaçoa. He was then thirty-two years of age, a fiery, valorous young soldier, who took pleasure in the pomp and display of military life, but, at the same time, was abundantly willing to share its toils and perils.

While commanding at Curaçoa, he headed an attempt to capture the island of St. Martin from the Portuguese—an attempt which his enemies called rash and his friends courageous. The attack failed, and the governor was so badly wounded as to lose one of his legs. In order to obtain better surgical treatment, he returned to Holland in 1644, where his leg was duly cared for, and his conduct at St. Martin's was pronounced by the company "a piece of Roman courage." The wooden leg which was made for him in Holland was adorned with bands of silver, which gave rise to the story that he wore a silver leg. Indeed the valiant governor was always fond of display. He was a man to decorate a wooden leg with bands of silver. He remained also a man of fiery temper, excessively fond of power, impatient of contradiction, and haughty in his demeanor. But he was honest, energetic, determined, and one of the bravest of the brave.

When he had recovered his health, he was rewarded for his past services by being appointed governor of the company's colony in New Netherland, the capital of which was New Amsterdam, upon Manhattan Island. The colony was not in a satisfactory condition. A bloody Indian war had laid waste many a flourishing farm, and bereaved many a worthy family; and this war had been needlessly provoked, and cruelly mismanaged. The colonists were oppressed with taxes, and yet the treasury was empty. They were discontented and discouraged, and there was great need of a more competent governor,

Upon Christmas-day, 1646, with a fleet of four vessels, Governor Stuyvesant sailed for the New World. Upon his way he visited the Dutch West Indies, where he gave evidence of his haughty and resolute disposition. A captured prize was to be disposed of, and the treasurer of the fleet demanded a seat at the counsel table where the affair was to be discussed. The governor repelled him, saying, " When I want you I will call you."

Some time after the officer renewed his claim, when the governor denied it more roughly than before, and would not permit him to put his foot on shore during the whole three weeks of his stay at the island of Curaçoa.

On the 11th of May, 1647, six months after his departure from Holland, Governor Stuyvesant's fleet entered the beautiful harbor of New Amsterdam, and anchored near the shore of Manhattan Island, then clad in the emerald freshness of spring. It was a joyful day to the inhabitants, who all turned out to greet the Governor at his landing, with arms in their hands. There was so much firing on the occasion, that almost all the powder in the town was wasted. As he assumed command, he said to the people, in his bluff, soldier-like way :

" I shall govern you as a father his children, for the advantage of the chartered West India Company, and these burghers and this land."

These words, and the frank bearing of the silver-legged soldier who uttered them, heightened the general enthusiasm, and the people went to their homes full of joyous expectations of a happier future.

At that time the city of New Amsterdam contained about ninety houses and seven or eight hundred inhabitants. There were laid out about a dozen streets, none of which were yet paved, and a good price for a building lot of an acre was forty dollars. The rent of the best house in the city would not have exceeded twelve dollars a year. The whole town was below Wall Street, and yet a large part of even that small territory was gardens and orchards. Every family kept its cow or cows, which were driven to the common pasture, out of town, by the public herdsman, who collected the cows from house to house, blowing a horn to give notice of his approach. He drove them by way of Pearl Street, then called Cow Path, to the site of the present City Hall Park, and this is the reason, it is said, why Pearl Street is so crooked.

The joy of the inhabitants at the coming of Governor Stuyvesant was not of long duration. His demeanor became exceedingly haughty. He kept some of the leading men of the city, who paid him a complimentary visit, waiting for several hours bareheaded, while he kept his hat on, says an old document, " as if he were the Czar of Muscovy." Besides this, he played the part of New Broom with disagreeable energy. He was one of those governors who take particular pleasure in issuing a proclamation. We have a long proclamation of his, published soon after his arrival, in which innkeepers were forbidden to sell liquor on Sundays before two o'clock in the afternoon, and after nine in the evening. Being a rigid Calvinist, he forbade pleasure-seeking on Sundays, and looked after the morals of the people as though they were indeed his children. On the other hand, he wisely forbade the selling of liquor to the Indians, and made it a capital offense to sell fire-arms to them. The Dutch at Albany had done great harm by selling guns to the Five Nations, and Peter Stuyvesant did his best to put an end to the traffic.

To replenish the treasury, he put in force an excise upon wine and liquor, increased the export duty upon furs, and collected arrears of taxes. In the hope of making a capture or two, he sent two small vessels to the West Indies in quest of the rich treasure-ships going home to Spain. He had the fences repaired, some of the streets straightened, and the general appearance of the town improved. Soon after his arrival he joined the church, caused the church edifice to be completed, and established over it a clergyman who had come with him from Curaçoa to Holland, and from Holland to America.

But with all this, he became more and more unpopular; for he was a soldier, and he had no other notion of government except that of absolute command and unquestioning obedience. The leading men desired the misconduct of Stuyvesant's predecessor to be investigated; but he would not permit it.

" If this point be conceded," said he, " will not these cunning fellows claim, in consequence, even greater authority against *ourselves* and *our* commission, should it happen that our administration may not square in every respect with their whims?"

So, instead of bringing the ex-governor to trial, he banished his accusers. He also gave an indignant refusal to those who claimed the right of appeal to the home government.

" If any one," he declared, " during my administration, shall appeal, I will make him a foot shorter, and send the pieces to Holland, and let him appeal in that way."

This was carrying it with a high hand; but the fiery old soldier found at last that he could not govern a colony in the wilderness as he would a regiment of soldiers in garrison at home. Money still refused to flow into the treasury; the Spanish prizes did not come in; the people evaded unpopular taxes; the Indians again threatened war. In these circumstances, the governor was obliged to allow the people a voice in the government, and a colonial legislature of nine members was summoned. This was the beginning of better days, for it appeased the general discontent, and the people paid more willingly the taxes imposed by their own representatives.

Stuyvesant's Indian policy was pacific and wise. But during a short absence of the governor, sixty-four canoes full of Indian warriors, numbering two thousand, landed one morning upon Manhattan Island before the dawn of day, and went all over the town, pretending to be in search of some of their own tribe. Their real object was to avenge the death of a squaw whom one of the townsmen had shot as she was stealing his peaches. The colonists rushed to arms, and succeeded at last in driving them to their canoes and over the river. But in Hoboken, Staten Island, and elsewhere the savages killed a hundred of the settlers, took a hundred and fifty prisoners, and laid waste twenty-eight farms. The governor hurried home and put the province in a posture of defense; but, at the same time, he used all his arts to conciliate the Indians. He managed so well that in a few days they gave up their prisoners, and made a treaty of peace.

From this time the colony prospered exceedingly. Emigrants arrived in greater numbers; a city government was organized; and the vigorous measures of the governor bore fruit. For seventeen years Peter Stuyvesant ruled the province of New Netherland. In 1664 a new danger threatened. England, which had always regarded the Dutch as trespassers upon this coast, now prepared to enforce its claim. Charles II. had made a present of this Dutch province to his brother, the Duke of York, and sent a fleet of four ships and four hundred and fifty troops to take possession. It was useless to resist, for the fort was defenseless against artillery.

"I would much rather be carried out dead," said the governor, "than surrender the place."

Upon reflection, however, he yielded, and on the eighth of September, 1664, marched out of the fort at the head of his little garrison, with drums beating and banners flying. The British flag was hoisted, and New Amsterdam became New York.

After the surrender, he went to his farm, three miles out of town, where he lived to the age of eighty, highly respected by his fellow-citizens. A portion of this farm remains to this day the property of his descendants; and, during the last forty years, it has so increased in value as to enrich a large circle of Stuyvesants and their connections. The stately mansion of Mr. Hamilton Fish, who is connected with the family by marriage, stands upon part of this estate. The old pear-tree brought by Governor Stuyvesant from Holland in 1647, and planted by his own hands, stood until a few years ago, when it was knocked down by a heavy load of timber. From its ancient root, however, a vigorous young shoot is springing, and promises to carry down the memory of Peter Stuyvesant for two centuries more. His remains repose in the family vault under St. Mark's Church, Second Avenue, upon the wall of which the original tablet may still be read:

In this vault lies buried
PETRUS STUYVESANT,
Late Captain-General and Commander-in-Chief
of Amsterdam, in New Netherland,
Now called New York,
And the Dutch West India Islands.
Died, August, A.D. 1682,
Aged 80 years.

SIR WILLIAM JOHNSON.

HE must be a dull traveler indeed who can ride through
the valley of the Mohawk, on the cars of the New York
Central railroad, with indifference. The mere beauty of the
scene, in the summer time, captivates the eye. At some
points the valley narrows to the breadth of a few miles,
through which the limpid Mohawk winds its way; while
near it the Erie canal, with numerous, slow-moving barges,
gives life and interest to the picture.

The view is bounded on one side by abrupt and lofty
hills, covered in some places with the primeval woods, down
which, in the spring, foaming torrents rush headlong to the
river. At other places, the forest has long since been shorn
away, and cattle are feeding on the smooth summits of the
hills almost directly above the traveler's head. The valley
itself, which is level almost to flatness, is of such fertility,
that after a hundred and fifty years of culture, it still produces the most luxuriant crops of broom-corn, maize, and
grain.

A great part of this beautiful valley, the value of which is
now almost incalculable, was, in 1734, given as the marriage
portion of a young lady of the city of New York—the
daughter of a noted man of that day, Etienne DeLancey—
when she married Admiral Sir Peter Warren of the British
navy. After his marriage, the Admiral added to his posses-
sions in the Mohawk valley by purchase, until he was the
possessor of the greater portion of the valley. The whole
region was then an unbroken wilderness, except where the
Indians had cleared a few acres for their corn-fields.

Admiral Warren had an Irish nephew named William
Johnson, born in County Meath in 1715, something of a
scapegrace, who at the age of nineteen fell in love with a

young lady who was no fit match for a wild young Irishman without property. Disappointed in love—so runs the tradition—he lent a willing ear to the proposal of his uncle, the Admiral, that he should cross the ocean, and see what he could do with this vast, unproductive Mohawk estate.

In 1738 he settled at a place twenty-four miles from Schenectady, to which Sir Peter had given the name of Warrensburg. For once, here was the right man in the right place. In person young Johnson was tall, straight, and strong, and his countenance had an expression of manly gravity which was both winning and commanding. There was much in him both of good and evil. He was honest, brave, and eloquent; but he was vain, boastful, and licentious. He possessed a singular talent for adapting himself to every situation and company in which he found himself. With gentlemen he was a gentleman; with Indians an Indian; and he could booze familiarly with the Albany Dutchmen, who at first were the only white neighbors he had. If he attended an Indian council, he was not too squeamish to eat dogs' flesh, or dance with the warriors, or flirt with the Indian girls; but when the council was in session, he knew how to assume that dignified bearing and to pour forth the flowery eloquence in which Indians delighted.

He excelled, too, in those sports and feats of agility upon which both Indians and white men at that time set so high a value. He joined in the Indians' ball play; he was a good hunter; he had, in short, every quality of manhood which either the red or the white inhabitants of the Mohawk valley could appreciate. At the same time, who cared for his faults? Indeed, it perhaps enhanced his influence, that, after the early death of his wife—a German girl of the neighborhood—he took mistress after mistress, now Dutch, now Indian. The last of them, an Indian girl named Molly Brant, bore him eight children.

He did great things with his uncle's Mohawk lands, assisted by his uncle's capital. He carried on an extensive trade with the Indians, acquiring over them a wonderful ascendency by his just dealing and easy manners. He observed two rules: 1. Never to deal with the Indians except when they were sober; and, 2. Always to fulfill his promise with exactness. If he once said No, he never yielded to their solicitations; and when he had said Yes, he would keep his word, at whatever loss or inconvenience to himself. All the Indians of the valley soon came to know this, and there is no virtue which an Indian more values. He soon became an adept in all the dialects of the region, and he frequently appeared among the Indians wearing their dress, which gave them particular delight. Of all the white men who ever had to do with the children of the forest, no one has ever wielded over them an influence so unbounded as William Johnson of New York.

When he had been five years in the country, war broke out between the French and English, and it became a matter of the utmost importance to keep the powerful tribes of New York faithful to their alliance with the English. It was William Johnson who frustrated at every point the machinations of the French, and held firm the unstable minds of the red men. Appointed by the government superintendent of Indian affairs, he usually wore the dress of an Indian chief, and visited all the tribes of the Six Nations, distributing liberal gifts, and pronouncing eloquent harangues. The result was, that the whole of the great province of New York remained unmolested and at peace. At the outbreak of this war, he built and fortified that large stone house, opposite Warrensburg, which is still standing and in good preservation.

From this time to the end of his life, he was generally in the public service, but continued actively to push his private fortune. He encouraged many families from the Highlands of Scotland and the North of Ireland to emigrate and settle on his lands, to whom he let farms on easy terms. He mentions, in one of his letters of 1763, that his tenantry consisted of one hundred and twenty families.

The old French war broke out in 1754. Again Johnson was placed at the head of the affairs of the Six Nations, and again he kept them faithful to their allegiance. Appointed a major general at the same time, he led a little army of hunters and farmers against Crown Point. Before he had reached it, he was most vigorously attacked by the French army, who at first gained an advantage which would have been decisive if Johnson's army had been regular troops. Instead of running away when they had been defeated, every man took to his tree or rock or shelving bank, and kept up a fire upon the French regulars which they could not return with any effect. The French continued to advance, however, until they came to where General Johnson had thrown up a hasty and rude breastwork of logs, from which the French tried in vain to dislodge him. When the enemy faltered and began to retreat, Johnson and his hunting-shirted farmers took the offensive, and drove back the Frenchmen with terrible slaughter.

It was for this victory that General Johnson was created a baronet, and rewarded by Parliament with a gift of five thousand pounds sterling. The king—George II.—made him a colonel in the British army, and permanent superintendent of Indian affairs at a salary of six hundred pounds sterling per annum, which he enjoyed for the rest of his life.

A few days before this battle, he named the beautiful sheet of water on the shore of which it was fought, Lake George, "not only," as he said, "in honor of his Majesty, but to assert his undoubted dominion here." The old French name was Lac Sacrement. He served, at the head of Indians and militia, to the end of the war, rendering essential aid at some of the most critical affairs. He was present with his Indian allies when Montreal and all Canada were surrendered to the English. Upon the return of peace the king granted him an additional reward of a hundred thousand acres in the State of New York.

At the time of Pontiac's Conspiracy in 1763, Sir William Johnson, for the third time, kept the Six Nations quiet, and restored the panic-stricken settlers to confidence. From this time to the beginning of the Revolutionary War he lived the life of a great frontier lord, dispensing the profuse hospitality, both to white men and Indians, which was then so much admired. In 1764, just after the Pontiac war, he built Johnson Hall, a large frame building, in which he passed the rest of his days, and which is still standing. Around this spacious residence he laid out the village still known by the name of Johnstown, now the county town of Fulton county. The Episcopal church there, which is still used, was built by Sir William. An officer who visited him in 1765, made this entry in his diary concerning his visit:

"*July* 11, 1765. Dined with Sir William at Johnson Hall. The office of superintendent very troublesome. Sir William continually plagued with Indians about him—generally from 300 to 900 in number—spoil his garden and keep his house always dirty."

This remarkable man was fortunate in the time of his death. If he had lived another year, he would have been compelled to take sides in the great controversy between the Colonies and the mother country, and the probability is, that, like most other persons who held office under the Crown, he would have taken the wrong side. He was spared this misfortune by dying in 1774. The old tradition that his death was hastened by the conflict of feeling in his own mind on this subject, may have had some foundations in truth, although the best investigators have rejected it.   His son, Sir John Johnson, joined the British forces, and lost his estates in consequence.   He died at Montreal, in 1830, aged eighty-eight.

JAMES LOGAN,
PENN'S PRIVATE SECRETARY.

AN anecdote which James Logan used to relate to his circle of friends in Philadelphia, gives us the key to his character.

He was crossing the Atlantic in the year 1699, with William Penn, whose secretary he then was.   He was a native of the north of Ireland, where his father, a man of learning, and educated for the Presbyterian church, became an early convert to the Quakers, and taught for many years a large school belonging to that society.   In this school, and under his father's tuition, James Logan was early imbued with a love of learning and science, and had acquired at the age of thirteen a proficiency in the ancient languages which was considered remarkable.   He afterward pursued mathematical studies with great success, and became himself a teacher of a grammar-school.   Few young men of his time were more accomplished than he; since, in addition to his classical and mathematical acquirements, he possessed a knowledge of French, Italian and Spanish.

Being a member of the Society of Friends, he was thrown into contact with William Penn, one of the great lights of that denomination, by whom he was invited to go out with him to Pennsylvania, as his secretary and man of business.   At that time pirates and privateers frequently assailed merchant vessels.   The ship in which Penn and

Logan were passengers being chased by an armed vessel, all the Quakers went below, as it is a tenet of their creed not to fight, even in self-defense. But James Logan, a robust and brave young fellow of twenty-five, proved himself on this occasion to be a better man than Quaker, and took his place at one of the guns to aid in beating off the expected enemy. But the armed ship, on coming up, proved to be a friendly vessel; upon learning which, Logan went into the cabin to communicate the joyful news. William Penn, then relieved of his apprehensions, began to scold Logan for his inconsistency in being willing to defend the ship. But Logan said:

"I being thy servant, William, why did not thee order me to come below? But thee was willing enough that I should stay and help fight the ship when thee thought there was danger."

William Penn's reply to this home-thrust is not recorded; but the young man did not forget the lesson; and in his subsequent transactions in connection with Pennsylvania affairs, he evidently bore the incident in mind.

Philadelphia in 1699 was a straggling village on the banks of the Delaware, fourteen years old, of two or three thousand inhabitants, though the province was rapidly filling up with immigrants. Penn soon returned to England, leaving Logan in charge of his interests, and manager of his estate—his agent and representative in all things. And Logan it was who had to bear the brunt of the ceaseless opposition of the colonists to the unwise, if not unjust, exactions of the Penn family. It was he, too, who conducted the negotiations with the Indians. He had much to do with a famous and powerful Mingo chief, named Shickelleny, upon whom Logan's exact justice and thoughtful humanity made such an impression that he named his son Logan; and this was that eloquent Logan whose speech, preserved by Mr. Jefferson, still figures in many of our school-books.

A world of trouble the agent had in pacifying the colonists and maintaining the rights of the proprietor. Many of the emigrants "squatted" upon land in the interior, and appeared to be exceedingly astonished when the agent demanded pay for the same; while others went through the form of purchase, took possession of their lands, and did not meet their engagements. The simple truth is: they were all farmers, and all raised wheat or tobacco, of which they produced so much that there was a glut in America of wheat, and of tobacco in England. The people had everything in abundance except money, and the few much-desired articles which could only be bought with money. In one of his letters, written when he had been a few years in the country, Logan uses such expressions as these:

"The tenants make my life so uncomfortable that it is not worth the living. . . . I know not what any of the comforts of life are. . . . Money is so scarce that many good farmers now scarce ever see a piece-of-eight of their own throughout the year. . . . What little there is of money is in town; and wheat, for two years past, has been worth very little. . . . Pay for land near New Castle, to the amount of three thousand pounds, is due, and I have received but two hundred pounds, and that in produce."

William Penn, although he had a large estate in England, was brought so heavily in debt by his province of Pennsylvania, that he had scarcely money enough to subsist upon, and was in danger of bankruptcy.

"Oh, Pennsylvania!" he once exclaimed, "what hast thou cost me? Surely above thirty thousand pounds more than ever I got by thee."

He expected results from his venture too soon. If he could have waited a few years longer, he would have had in

Pennsylvania a valuable estate, which his sons enjoyed and grossly abused down to the time of the Revolution. In due time Logan laid down his agency and entered into private business, seriously intending to acquire a respectable estate of his own. He once gave the reason of this determination, which may be worth considering.

"When I was a young man," he wrote, "and secretary to Penn, I felt an indifference to money, and deemed this a happy retirement for cultivating the Christian graces. But after I had had some experience in life, finding how little respect and influence could be usefully exerted without such competency as could give a man ready access to good society, I thenceforward set myself seriously to endeavor, by engagements in commerce (a new track to me), to attain that consequence and weight which property so readily confers."

In this he succeeded. He soon gained a considerable estate, which enabled him to serve the colonies in important offices, and to spend the evening of his days in the pursuit of knowledge.

It was not until he was approaching three score years and ten that he had occasion to put in practice the lesson which he had learned of William Penn, on his passage across the sea; since Pennsylvania, during the first sixty-five years of its existence as a colony, enjoyed peace with all the world. In 1744, England being involved in war with great powers in Europe, the colonies were threatened with attack, and New England was engaged in active hostilities against the French in Canada. Privateers ravaged the seas, and the cities on the coast were filled with apprehensions of the enemy's fleets. Philadelphia was without defense of any kind. There was not a fort, nor a battery, nor an earthwork, nor a cannon, nor a volunteer company, nor muskets enough to arm one, nor any beginning of a militia system.

One stout pirate could have sailed up the Delaware and laid Philadelphia under contribution.

Benjamin Franklin, bookseller and postmaster, wrote an artful and powerful pamphlet calling upon the people to organize for the defense of their homes and families. In a few days ten thousand men in the province had joined the proposed organization, and nothing was thought of but muskets and batteries, drilling and parades. The Quakers were in a terrible dilemma between their sectarian principles and the instincts of human nature. James Logan and some others openly sided with Franklin, declaring that self-defense was equally the dictate of nature and religion. Logan, too old to serve in the field, subscribed five hundred pounds for the purchase of cannon, besides affording Franklin all the support of his influence and reputation.

"A Government without arms is an inconsistency," he wrote to Franklin.

The great body of the Quakers, however, were more disposed, as Mr. Logan remarked, to *get* estates than to defend them. Some of the young men resorted to an artifice in order to contribute money for the defense of the town without offending their elders. They agreed to raise money for "a fire-engine," and to intrust the same to Benjamin Franklin, who proceeded to buy with it a great gun, "which," said he, with a twinkle in his eye, "is certainly a *fire-engine.*"

Fortunately, the enemy did not attempt to enter the Delaware river, and the aged philosopher was soon enabled to resume his studies. Franklin, during this very year, 1744, published Logan's excellent translation of Cicero's discourse upon old age, with an interesting preface by Franklin himself, which continued to be republished in England and Scotland for many years after the translator's death. Several other works of science and scholarship he produced at this period of his life, and he gathered round him at his country-seat near Germantown an excellent library and a valuable collection of objects relating to science. He was the venerated chief of that small circle of scholars and philosophers of which Franklin was the active and informing spirit, into which Rittenhouse and Rush were afterward admitted, and who will forever make the early history of Pennsylvania an essential part of the annals of mankind. Such men as Franklin, Logan and Rittenhouse are the only permanent glory of a State.

James Logan died in 1751, aged seventy-seven years. His remains lie buried in the Arch street ground belonging to the Friends. His name and family are still among the most honored in Pennsylvania.

Captain Kid and the Pirates.

From an early period in the history of New England the coast was infested with pirate vessels. As early as 1632 we hear of a man named Dixy Bull who turned pirate and plundered the towns on the coast and the fishermen near it. Governor Winthrop sent a pinnace in pursuit of him, which cruised two months without success, and the pirate afterward got safely to England, where he died a violent death. For a hundred years after no ship approached the coast, nor left it, without keeping a bright look-out for pirates, and few seasons passed without ships being captured by these high-waymen of the sea.

In that age wars were frequent between Holland, France, England, and Spain. No sooner was war declared than privateering licenses were issued, and the more adventurous sailors were eager to take advantage of them, and scour the sea in quest of rich prizes. Landsmen, too, used to club together, buy a vessel, arm and equip her as a privateer, and send her to sea in command of some daring captain noted for his success in this kind of warfare. Occasionally a splendid prize was brought in, which would enrich the adventurers, and give a great impulse to the business. As long as the war lasted, and as long as the privateers confined their attacks to the enemy's ships, no one objected. But when peace returned, there was a large body of men, afloat and ashore, who had been demoralized by the roving, reckless life of a privateer, and who were not at all disposed to settle down again into the humdrum life of good citizens, or to be satisfied with the regular gains of ordinary seamanship. Many of these men became pirates, and preyed upon the increasing commerce between Europe and America.

Ships upon the ocean were then few and far between, and in time of peace there were few men-of-war serving as the police of the sea. The consequence was, that a pirate ship of some magnitude, well-manned and well-armed, usually had everything its own way for a time, and captured every vessel it overtook.

The success of some noted pirates gave such a powerful stimulus to the business that there appeared, at length, some danger of the total extinction of honest commerce. In one of the letters of that learned and excellent Philadelphia Quaker, James Logan, written in 1717, there is a remarkable passage, which shows how numerous the pirates had become on our coast :

"We have been extremely pestered with pirates," he writes, "who now swarm in America, and increase their numbers by almost every vessel they take. If speedy care be not taken they will become formidable, being *now at least fifteen hundred strong.* They have very particularly talked of visiting this place, many of them being very well ac-

quainted with it, and some born in it; for they are generally all Englishmen, and therefore know our government can
make no defense."

Philadelphia was then only thirty-two years old, and being inhabited chiefly by Quakers, could have offered little re-
sistance to a pirate fleet manned by fifteen hundred sailors.
In that same year, 1717, there was one week in October,
Mr. Logan mentions, when the pirates took and plundered,
in the Delaware, six or seven vessels! Some Philadelphians,
who were taken prisoners, heard them say that they had
eight hundred men in Rhode Island, and another band in
North Carolina, all under the command of one captain. The
pirate vessel which made those captures had a crew of one
hundred and thirty men, " all stout fellows," says Logan,
" all English and doubly armed." They said that they were
only waiting for their consort of twenty-six guns to attack
and plunder Philadelphia. Nor was this a mere momentary
or occasional panic, for a year after the same James Logan
wrote :

" We are now sending down a small vessel to seize those
rogues, if not strengthened from sea. We are in manifest
danger here, unless the king's ships take some notice of us.
It is possible, indeed, that the merchants of New York,
some of them I mean, might not be displeased to hear we
are all reduced to ashes. Unless these pirates be deterred
from coming up our rivers by the fear of men-of-war outside
to block them in, there is nothing but what we may fear
from them."

The danger was all the greater, because some of the
merchants and contractors, who had fitted out privateers
during the war, continued to supply the same vessels, when,
at the return of peace, they had turned pirates. Sometimes,
indeed, the pirate ships were strong enough to hold their
own against a man-of-war. In the year 1723, for example,

two pirate vessels came in near Sandy Hook when a British man-of-war was going out of New York harbor. After a desperate fight, the smaller of the pirates was taken, and the whole crew of forty-two men were hanged in a row on Long Island. But the other escaped, and made twenty prizes before she was caught. In the same year, 1723, twenty-six pirates were hanged at Newport, Rhode Island. Indeed, it was a common event, about that time, for pirates to be strung up in a row in that wholesale fashion; for, by this time, the British government had begun to bestir itself and put forth systematic efforts for the suppression of piracy.

Captain Robert Kid, born about 1650, was for many years a resident of the city of New York, where he had a wife and child, and whence he sailed, for several years, as a respectable merchant captain and privateersman. So highly was he esteemed, that no man's services were in so much request among the merchants of New York, and every one was eager for shares in a privateer which he was to command. Among the old records of the city of New York his name frequently occurs. Sometimes he is mentioned as demanding the return of one of his sailors who had been impressed into the king's service, and sometimes as bringing in a prize, and paying to the king the tenth and to the governor the fifteenth which the law allowed them.

About 1695 the piracies on the American coast had become so numerous, and so destructive of commerce, that a kind of society was formed in England, headed by the king, William III., for their suppression. The company fitted out and armed a ship of thirty guns, named the "Adventure," designing that she should pursue and capture the pirates, and sell their vessels for the advantage of the company. When the ship was getting ready for sea, it so happened that Colonel Robert Livingston, of New York, a member of the well-known New York family of that name, was in London. Colonel Livingston not only recommended Captain Kid for the command of this vessel, but engaged to become his security for the faithful performance of his duty. He spoke of Captain Kid as a "bold and honest man," well fitted to suppress the piracies in the American seas. The appointment was accordingly given to Kid, and he received the king's commission, which was directed "to the trusty and beloved Captain Kid." Bearing this commission, he sailed from Plymouth in 1696, and bore away for the American coast.

Probably the pirates took the alarm ; for he cruised for several months between Boston and Virginia without making important captures. Occasionally he visited New York harbor, anchoring off the Battery, and while there, took pains to enlist a daring and numerous crew, until, at last, he had a resolute band of a hundred and fifty men. Toward the close of 1696 he struck across the Atlantic, bound for the East Indies, and on the way made known to his crew that he meant to turn pirate, and dash in among the richly freighted ships of the Eastern seas. The men offering no effective opposition, he continued his course around the Cape of Good Hope, and made his way to the Red Sea, where he began his depredations. He captured many vessels, gaining, as is supposed, a prodigious booty, and at length took a merchant ship of four hundred tons, laden with precious merchandise.

With this vessel, and a vast amount of gold and silver and precious stones, he started on his return to America. The large ship he gave up to one of his band, and in his own vessel he returned to our waters, and buried a large amount of treasure on Gardner's Island, near the end of Long Island. A portion of this, and perhaps all of it, was afterward found by Lyon Gardner, the owner of the island, who surrendered it to the governor of Massachusetts :

namely, three bags of gold dust, containing about one hundred and fifty ounces, two bags of golden bars, weighing nearly six hundred ounces, two or three bags of precious stones, and several of broken silver. It is possible that he buried treasure at other places on the coast.

Having secured so much treasure, the next thing to consider was how he could get on shore to enjoy it. The Earl of Bellemont, governor of Massachusetts, was one of the stockholders in the original enterprise, and Kid, presuming upon this fact, sent one of his men to Boston to learn from the governor what treatment he might expect if he should go ashore. The governor, it appears, replied in language which admitted of two interpretations, one favorable to Kid's hopes, and the other not. He went to Boston, and appeared openly in the streets, where he was at once arrested. He was sent to England for trial, but it was difficult to convict him of piracy, owing to the commission which he bore ; and after a long delay, he was arraigned on a charge of murdering one of his crew, and condemned to die. Col. Livingston, of New York, who owned one fifth of the vessel in which Kid had sailed, befriended him to the last. He was hanged at Execution Dock, in London, March 23, 1701.

For many years after his death, people living along the coast of Long Island could not quite get it out of their heads that Kid had buried vast treasures there, and they spent a great deal of time in digging for them. The song of Captain Kid, written soon after his execution, continues to the present day to be popular among sailors, and you may often hear it sung in the evening on the forecastle of ships:

> My name was Captain Kid,
> When I sailed, when I sailed ;
> My name was Captain Kid,
> And so wickedly I did,

God's laws I did forbid,
When I sailed, when I sailed.

I roamed from Sound to Sound,
And many a ship I found,
And them I sunk or burned,
When I sailed, when I sailed.

Farewell to young and old,
All jolly seamen bold;
You are welcome to my gold,
For I must die, I must die.

Farewell, for I must die;
Then to eternity,
In hideous misery,
I must lie, I must lie.

Every sailor, however, has his own version of the song, and sings as many stanzas as the patience of his hearers will endure.

Samuel Parris, and the Salem Witchcraft.

Samuel Parris was the minister of the church in Salem, Massachusetts, in 1692, when the events occurred which are usually spoken of as the Salem witchcraft. He was a man of much talent as a preacher and composer of extempore prayers; but by his arrogance and vanity he had estranged so many of his flock, that he was in danger of dismission. He had not been regularly trained to the ministry. He had been for some years a merchant, and he had brought with him from the West Indies several slaves, whom he continued to hold and employ after his settlement in the ministry. These negroes, besides being themselves superstitious, as all ignorant people are, had lived among Spaniards, who in that age were noted for their unquestioning belief in witchcraft.

For four years, Cotton Mather's sermon narrating the ingenious tricks of four Boston children, supposed to be bewitched, had been circulating in Massachusetts. Nothing is more remarkable in children than their propensity to imitate; and it came to pass, in the winter of 1691 and 92, that some girls in Salem took it into their heads to repeat the antics described in Dr. Mather's sermon, which had deceived the wise men of Boston, and made such a stir throughout America. Living near the residence of the minister, Samuel Parris, these girls had been accustomed to talk with his slaves about witches and witchcraft, and it is probable that their interest in the subject had been much increased thereby. However that may be, these girls, six or seven in number, the youngest nine and the oldest eighteen, fell into the habit of coming together at the minister's house and elsewhere, for the express purpose of practicing the devices which they had learned from Cotton Mather's sermon, or from the servants' conversation, or from both.

After practicing a while in secret, they began, before the winter ended, to perform in the presence of others. They would cry out without any obvious cause, twist their bodies, creep into holes, get under chairs, throw themselves into unnatural postures, gesticulate wildly, and utter incoherent sounds. Sometimes they would pretend to be seized with spasms, fall senseless to the floor, or writhe about and shriek, as if in agony. Scarcely a creature in the town appears to have doubted, for one moment, that these antics were involuntary. The children were regarded with the tenderest compassion, as undergoing unaccountable and horrible suffering.

The physician of the place was called in. A consultation was held, and the children were pronounced bewitched.

It was not unusual, in that credulous age, for doctors to give opinions of this nature. When their science did not avail, and a patient grew worse, it was consolatory to their self-love, and beneficial to their reputation, to say that the sick person was afflicted by an Evil Spirit; and no explanation of a mysterious malady was so readily believed as that.

The girls, finding themselves objects of so much attention, rose with the occasion. When people flocked in from the country to witness their supposed torments, they exerted themselves to vary and intensify the exhibition. They began at length to cry out in church-time, using such expressions as, "Look where she sits upon the beam, sucking her yellow-bird betwixt her fingers." Or like this: "There is a yellow-bird sitting on the minister's hat, as it hangs on the pin in the pulpit!" Sometimes, just before the minister rose to preach, one would cry out, "Now stand up and name your text." If the sermon was long, one would say, perhaps, "Now there is enough of that," or words to similar effect.

No one thought of rebuking the girls for such conduct; for they were supposed to be under an influence which they could not resist, and they continued to be regarded with mingled awe, terror, and pity. Every one treated them with the greatest attention and tenderness. A few persons in the parish, it is true, soon recovered sense enough to disapprove the proceedings, and had the courage to absent themselves from church; but whoever held aloof was regarded by the church generally as in some degree countenancing the Evil One, and the minister, Samuel Parris, appears to have marked them for destruction.

The excitement was a godsend indeed to this artful, vain, and domineering clergyman. He was one of those persons who delight in being the center of a scene, or a ceremonial.

Power was dear to him for its own sake; and besides believing, as every one then believed, in the constant presence and habitual interference of evil spirits, he rejoiced in everything like commotion, excitement, and conflict. Restored by these events to more than his former popularity and power, he did all that was possible to foment the mischief, and he contrived, ere long, to use the prevailing mania as a means of intimidating his opponents.

His first step was to summon the clergy of the province to meet in council at his house. The children were brought in. They performed their antics as usual, while the reverend gentlemen looked on in silent amazement and horror. At length the ministers declared their belief that the Evil One had taken possession of the girls, and that he had begun his operations in Salem with a bolder front, and on a broader scale than ever before, in either the New or the Old World. When this decision of the council was made known, the community absolutely lost its senses. To use the language of Mr. Charles W. Upham of Salem, who spent many years in the investigation of this subject:

"Society was dissolved into a wild and excited crowd. Men and women left their fields, their houses, their labors, and employments, to witness the awful unveiling of the demoniac power, and to behold the workings of Satan himself upon the victims of his wrath."

And now the people began to ask, with a wild intensity of eagerness, WHO are the agents of the devil? WHO are the witches? The children were continually questioned: "WHO is it that bewitches you?" Soon they began to utter the names of poor, unfortunate women who had made themselves disagreeable to their neighbors. One was named Sarah Good, a forlorn, friendless, and forsaken woman. Another was Sarah Osburne, a woman in humble life, of respectable character, but connected with a family opposed to the minister of the parish. Another was a half idiotic slave, belonging to Parris.

In due time these three women were arrested, and arraigned with unusual solemnity and pomp, and each of them was subjected to a long examination.

"Sarah Good," said the magistrate, "what evil spirit have you familiarity with?"

She replied: "None."

"Have you made no contracts with the devil?"

"No."

"Why do you hurt these children?"

"I do not hurt them. I scorn it."

"Who do you employ, then, to do it?"

"I employ nobody."

The magistrate then told the children to look at her, and see if this was the person who tormented them, and they all answered that she was the one who did so. Upon this they all pretended to be tormented, and performed their accustomed writhing and outcries. When the prisoner had again protested her innocence, the magistrate asked her:

"Whom do you serve?"

"I serve God."

"What God do you serve?"

"The God that made heaven and earth."

Sarah Osburne also declared her innocence, and so did the slave. The slave, however, pretended to be herself bewitched, and showed much cunning in making the people believe that she was one of the victims, instead of one of the guilty. This woman said, after the excitement was over, that her master had beaten her and compelled her to accuse of witchcraft such persons as he designated. After remaining in prison a year, she was sold to pay her jail fees. Sarah Osburne died in prison after several weeks' confinement. Sarah Good lay in jail chained and bound with cords.

The children and their confederates, emboldened by success, began now to accuse persons of more importance in the community, selecting most of their victims from families opposed to the minister. The trials went on until five women were in Salem jail, who had been tried and found guilty of witchcraft. All of them were executed on the same day, and all of them were as innocent of harming the children as their own mothers.

This wholesale execution served but to increase the excitement. The clergy still preached alarming sermons upon the subject, urging the magistrates to go on in the work of warring against the devil by destroying his agents. During the whole summer of 1692 the madness raged. Five were executed in July, five in August, and in September the astonishing number of *eight* virtuous and exemplary persons were conveyed in one cart to the top of a hill in Salem and hanged together.

But this awful scene closed the tragedy; for the Governor, Sir William Phips, interfered, discharged all the remaining prisoners, and terminated the proceedings. During the prevalence of the mania, several hundreds of people had been committed to prison, none of whom were released until they had paid jail fees, court fees, and their board during confinement. Twenty were executed, several died in jail, and a great many families lost all their property.

With returning reason, Samuel Parris became more odious than before, and although the conservative party in the church supported him to the last, he was ejected at length, and spent the remainder of his days in poverty and obscurity. Eighteen years after the legislature of Massachusetts declared all the witchcraft judgments and convictions null and void, and voted nearly six hundred pounds for distribution among the injured families.

Captain Henry Hudson's Trip to Albany in Search of the Pacific Ocean.

AMERICAN travelers and students have discovered much curious information in their researches among the archives and libraries of European capitals. Some years ago one of our historical students found, among the records, in Amsterdam, of the ancient Dutch East India Company, the "ship book" of the vessel in which Henry Hudson sailed up the noble river that now bears his name. It was in the service and at the expense of this East India Company that he made the voyage. The vessel was named the Half Moon, and she was of eighty tons burden—about as large as a good sized North river sloop. She was a vessel of two masts, and was built expressly for speed; being what we should now call a yacht. Her crew consisted of twenty men, some Dutch and some English. The mate was a Dutchman, and as she sailed under the Dutch flag and in the service of a Dutch company, whatever land she might discover would of course belong to Holland.

About sunset on the second of September, 1609, more than five months after leaving Amsterdam, Captain Hudson came in sight of those inviting headlands, now called the hills of Navesink, which so agreeably salute the arriving voyager as he approaches New York. Rejoicing in the prospect, he sailed on the next morning, and before night anchored inside of Sandy Hook, with the Narrows, leading into New York bay, straight before him. So pleased was he with the lands and waters about him, that he remained in the lower bay fishing and exploring for a week. Doubtless he or some of his men walked upon the beach at Long Branch ; and very pleasant it must have been to them in the bright, warm days of the first week in September. Every day the long-boat of the Half Moon was manned, and made long excursions in what we now call Raritan Bay, and round where Perth Amboy now stands, and up through the Narrows into the beautiful harbor with its exquisite shores and green islands. Hudson mentions in his Report, that the lands about our harbor, in their virgin freshness, were "as pleasant with grass and flowers and goodly trees" as any he had ever seen, and the breezes wafted from them sweet odors. Returning one evening from what we now call Newark Bay, the boat was attacked by two canoes full of Indians, and before they were driven off they killed one of the crew.

After sounding and exploring for a week, Captain Hudson ventured to hoist his anchor, and sail up through the Narrows as far as the opening of the strait between Staten Island and New Jersey, where again he dropped his anchor, and looked about him. Canoes full of Indians approached the vessel, making signs of friendship, and offering for sale oysters and beans. Captain Hudson would not permit any of them to come on board, but was glad enough to buy the excellent oysters which, at that day, as now, abounded in the kills between Staten Island and the other shore. The next morning a great fleet of canoes, twenty-eight in number, filled with men, women, and children, hovered about the vessel; but the captain feared to trust them, and let none of them come on board.

All that region swarmed with Indians; for the red man was an excellent judge of a country to live in. He required a place where land and water were conveniently blended, so that he could procure for his subsistence the products of both. Thus, in the early days, the Indian population was large in the valleys of great rivers like the Hudson, the Connecticut, the Potomac, the James, and the Mobile, and in such regions as Rhode Island, where sea and land are intermixed. Nowhere, perhaps, in the northern States were the Indians more numerous than in the valley of the Hudson; and the names of several of the tribes designate to this day the places which they inhabited. Our island, for example, was occupied by the Manhattans, and, thirty miles up the river, the Sait-Sings dwelt, whose name, corrupted to Sing Sing, is familiar to us all. On the other side of the river were the Hackensacks, and lower down in the bay the Raritans. The Indians on each side of the river were hereditary foes, frequently at war, although capable of uniting against the Five Nations in the interior of the State. Amid this numerous population, it was but natural that Captain Hudson, in his eighty ton vessel, and with his crew of twenty men, should proceed with caution.

After spending the morning in viewing the beautiful scene around him, and watching the Indian canoes which surrounded the vessel, he hoisted his anchor and sailed up the bay for six miles, and cast his anchor for the night opposite Manhattan Island. The next morning, seeing the broad river stretch before him as far as the eye could reach, he entertained the hope that now at last he had discovered a passage leading into the Pacific. The tide being favorable, he drifted up the stream all day, and dropped his anchor in the evening opposite to the site of the village of Yonkers. The next day, a southerly breeze springing up, and assisted also by the tide, the Half Moon was wafted so rapidly up the river, that when night fell she was in the midst of the grand scenery of the Highlands, and anchored not far from West Point.

The next day Captain Hudson was equally fortunate. It was one of those beautiful September days, hazy in the morning, but clear and bright soon after sunrise, which reveal the loveliness of nature with a mingled depth and brilliancy unknown at any other part of the year. I am sure, from the warmth of Captain Hudson's expressions, that he was a man to enjoy the glorious scene around him. On this day he made sixty miles, anchoring at night opposite Catskill, in full view of the mountains. By this time, it seems, he had changed his opinion of the natives; for the next morning, when they came off to the vessel, bringing tobacco, pumpkins, and the newly ripened ears of corn, he let them come on board, and bought from them those products of the country.

He lingered in that enchanting part of the river all the morning, amusing himself with the Indians, and admiring the picturesque magnificence of the view. In the afternoon he sailed six miles further, and anchored about opposite the site of the present city of Hudson. Beyond this point the navigation becomes more difficult; so that the next day he made only eighteen miles, stopping for the night near Castleton. The next morning he went ashore with an aged chief, who took him to his house and entertained him hospitably. It was a region, he says in his diary, flowing with abundance. The chief had enough corn and beans to load "three ships;" and two men who were sent out, as soon as he arrived, to kill him some game, brought in very soon a pair of pigeons. They also killed a fat dog, and dressed it with shells for his supper, supposing that he would remain all night.

" The land," he added, " is the finest for cultivation that I ever in my life set foot upon, and it also abounds in trees of every description. These natives are a very good people; for when they saw that I would not remain, they supposed that I was afraid of their bows; and, taking their arrows, they broke them in pieces and threw them into the fire."

Early the next morning he continued his voyage a few miles further, and anchored very nearly opposite where the city of Albany now stands. Here again the Indians came on board in great numbers, bringing corn, grapes, and pumpkins, as well as skins of beaver and otter. The vessel remained at this spot for several days, while the carpenter hewed from the forest a new foreyard. On one of these days the captain gave some of the principal chiefs so much wine and brandy that they were all half drunk. The poor Indians seem to have been entirely puzzled and confounded by the effects of the strange liquid.

The reader can imagine the amazement of the Indians along the banks of the Hudson, as the Half Moon made her way up the stream. The tradition of it lingered among their descendants for four generations: for we know that, about the year 1760, a Moravian missionary heard the tale related by aged Indians as they had received it from their fathers and grandfathers. A long time ago, they told him, some Indians who were out fishing in a wide part of the river espied at a great distance something enormous floating on the water, which they had never seen before. Going ashore, they told their friends of it, and urged them to paddle out into the stream and try to discover what it might be. They did so, and they all gazed at the strange thing, wondering what it was. Some said it was a huge fish or animal, and others thought it a large house. It was plain, however, that the tremendous object *moved*, and appeared to be moving toward the shore. So they sent runners in every direction to summon the chiefs and warriors. The object drew near. It was evidently an immense canoe or floating house, and they concluded that the Great Spirit was on board, and they made haste to prepare a great feast with which to regale him on his arrival. When the great canoe came up, a man with a white skin, and wearing a red garment, hailed them in a friendly manner. And so they went on relating the particulars of the interview, dwelling especially upon the delightful effects which followed the drinking of the white man's fire-water.

Above Albany, as most readers know, the Hudson is but a narrow and shallow stream. Captain Hudson now began to see very plainly that this beautiful stream was only a river of the country, and that he would never get to China by means of it. He sent a boat's crew to explore further, who went about ten miles above the present city of Troy, and brought back the report that the river was navigable no further. With great reluctance he turned his prow down the stream.

In the ascent of the river he had occupied eleven days, and he spent the same time in descending it, stopping often where he had stopped before, and detained sometimes by head winds. Near the mouth of the river he again found the Indians hostile. At the upper end of the island of Manhattan, near what we now call Fort Washington, several hundred Indians gathered to attack the vessel as she passed; but a single shot killing two of them, the rest took to flight. Soon after a large canoe full of warriors boldly attacked the Half Moon. Another shot from a small cannon stove and sunk the canoe, causing the death of nine of the Indians. He anchored that night near Hoboken, as far as he could get from the warlike Manhattans. A day or two after, exactly a month from the day of his arrival at Sandy Hook, he set sail again into the broad Atlantic.

Five weeks after he cast anchor in the English harbor of Dartmouth. He sent over a report of his discoveries to Amsterdam, and received orders from his company to bring his ship thither. Just as he was about to put to sea, he was stopped by the English government, and ordered not to leave England, since he owed his service to his own country. All the English part of his crew received the same orders, and several months passed before the Half Moon was permitted to return to Holland without her commander. Captain Hudson next sailed in the service of a London company, and made the voyage from which he never returned.

Mr. J. R. Brodhead, the historian of the State of New York, whose researches have rescued for us much of our early history that might otherwise never have come to light, has ascertained the subsequent fate of the Half Moon. In 1611 she was one of a fleet which sailed to the East Indies, and in the Indian Seas, in March, 1615, she was wrecked and lost. The river discovered by Hudson was named by the Dutch the *Mauritius*, but the name would not adhere, as all the rest of the world called it by the name of the discoverer.

www.ingramcontent.com/pod-product-compliance
Lightning Source LLC
Chambersburg PA
CBHW021527090426
42739CB00007B/812